Lincolns⊦

on old pict⊦

Eric

1. Brattleby. Mayple dancing on the lawn of Brattleby Hall. The card is unused but would appear to have been published about 1910.

Designed and published by
Reflections of a Bygone Age,
Keyworth, Nottingham 2003

Printed by Adlard Print &
Reprographics Ltd, Ruddington

£3.50

Introduction

When I compiled the book *Lincolnshire at Work* in 1995, I intended it should have a companion volume *Lincolnshire at Play*. Well, here it is - nine years later! In sorting out the postcards for this book, I was immediately struck by the lack of information on the cards. After giving it some thought, I came to the conclusion that it isn't all that surprising. Most of the cards are of special events and published by local photographers, or even amateurs, who didn't have the facility for titling the cards in the same way as commercial producers. They were often sold in small numbers in local shops, and perhaps mainly bought by the people who are in them. They didn't bother to write on the backs because they knew what the picture was about! A good many were never posted but kept as souvenirs of the event. If you think someone is going to be looking at your family photographs in 100 years time, then get writing on them now!

Most successful commercial postcards of personalities in the 1900-14 period featured famous ones: cricketers, actresses, royals, or politicians. The postcards in this book feature ordinary folk who attained permanent, if anonymous fame, by their appearance. It was the Edwardian equivalent of a brief TV exposure. Many local photographers deliberately tried to include as many folk as possible on their cards to help sales.

I have tried to feature as many types of events over as diverse an area of the county as the type of book and my collection will allow. This is not intended as any sort of history book, nor is it written with any authority on my part. It is a collection of Edwardian scenes that typify the feel of Lincolnshire towns and villages in the early 20th century.

Picture postcards were first published in Britain in 1894, but it was not until a decade later that they began to take off, when in 1902, the Post Office allowed a message to be written on the address side. This meant that the whole of one side was available for the picture and obviously this gave more scope to the publisher. Photographic viewcards became very popular and the postcard became the most important way of communicating news or messages, in much the same way as the telephone or emails are used today. The years up to 1914 were the *Golden Age* of picture postcards, when millions of imaginative designs covering every subject under the sun were published by a host of national and local firms. Where known, postcard publishers have been acknowledged.

I have purposely excluded most sporting events, as I hope one day to produce *Sport in Lincolnshire*.

Eric Croft
July 2004

Front cover: **Dunholme**, and a United Methodist Sunday School treat in 1912. The carts look a bit overcrowded but usually with these events, they were only travelling two or three miles. The card was published by JS Simnett of Burton-on-Trent.

Back cover (top): **Wellingore Feast 1906** by an unknown publisher. He obviously produced too many, as they were still on sale at New Year!

Back cover (bottom): **Keadby** about 100 years ago - *see illus. 8* for further details.

2. Grimsby. A car rally featured on a postcard published by Porri's News Bureau of Grimsby. Someone has written on the back *ARROL-JOHNSTON 1914*, which I assume is the make of car number 1.

3. Grimsby. A scene at the Gaiety Hall rink in Grimsby in 1922. All the children on the front row are wearing roller skates.

4. Cleethorpes. The Martin Aviation Co. organised an aerial joy ride, pictured on this postcard by local photograper JW Hardy. The chap in the middle is a kilted Scotsman, on the right there appears to be an ice cream man, so I assume the fellow on the left is the pilot!

5. Barrow-on-Humber boy scouts photographed by Barton photographer Bertram Parker. It hasn't been posted, but probably dates from the World War One period.

6. Grimsby. The banner to the left reads *Lincoln Diocese C.E.T.S. Challenge Band of Hope banner competition,* but gives no idea of the date.

YARBOROUGH PACK.
The Meet of the Hounds in Brigg Market Place, February 24th, 1905.

Jacksons,' Stationers, Brigg.

7. Brigg. Nothing much to add to this caption except that Brigg townsfolk obviously loved their hunting, as I doubt whether any of them are protestors!

8. Keadby about 100 years ago. This postcard probably features a Sunday School procession as the first cart has a piano on board! Plenty of flags are in evidence: even one of the three River Trent barges in the distance is sporting a flag of some sort, so it could be a regatta procession.

9. Brigg. This would appear to be the unveiling of the War Memorial or perhaps peace celebrations after World War One.

10. Owston Ferry. This card, published by Scrivens of Doncaster, shows a Trent Regatta c1905.

11. Crowle Market Place on a card by local photographer S. Couch and posted in 1907. There is an elephant - promoting a local circus entertainment - walking down the street, but apart from a few children, it isn't exactly drawing the crowds. Perhaps elephants were once common in Crowle!

12. Scunthorpe Charity Sports 14th August 1909, showing the start of the 12-mile race, described somewhat erroneously as a 'marathon'. The winner was apparently the chap in the striped shirt on the right. What a serious looking bunch!

13. Scunthorpe. The card bears the impressed stamp of Scunthorpe photographer Singleton. There are a few flags about and an enormous banner. In view of the crown in the car windscreen, the occasion could well be the coronation celebration of 1911.

14. A scene at **Barton-on-Humber,** but again with no clue to the event except that it is a pageant of some sort. The photographer was B. Parker of Barton.

15. Louth Market Place decorated for the Louth Show in 1909. They obviously put a lot of effort into the street decorations for the event.

16. Louth c1910. An anonymous, unused postcard, but someone has kindly written on the back *Louth King Edward VI School.* No wonder they look reluctant to dive in - the teacher is fully clothed, complete with overcoat, and huddled up against the fence!

17. South Elkington Fete on another undated, unused postcard but c1910. There are hundreds of people watching, just visible under the trees, so as the population of the village was only 350, the event drew people from far and wide!

18. North Thoresby Show on an undated card by WR Phillips of Fulstow. From the size of the crowds it was obviously an important event in the village calendar. The caption reads *Judging Class 19*. There appears to be only two horses, so at least they both got a prize!

19. Gainsborough Life Saving Chums 1927 seen posing with their trophy. I have not heard of this organisation, but they seem to be a cub/scout troop with two arkalas from the Salvation Army!

20. Scotter. P.M. Centenary Motor Car visiting Scotter on 1st October 1907. The car, which was for fund-raising (somehow), was irrelevant to these church elders. They look more like the Scotter mafia!

21. Owmby. The caption reads *Primrose Cycle Club at Owmby Rectory, Sunday 25th May 1913.* I have no idea what this is about, but I am certain they didn't arrive here on cycles in these clothes and hats!

22. Market Rasen Sports Day 1907, but that is all I know about it. I think the lady on the right won this egg and spoon race, unless she collided with the goal post!

23. Lincoln. Ruston Proctor Co works outing about 1910. The company hired a train to take its employees on the annual works outing, which included visits to Skegness and Matlock. Either the engine was a new one or had been spruced up for the occasion.

24. Lincoln. Theatrical performers like this eight-piece pierrot troupe often used picture postcards to promote their acts.

25. Lincoln. This magnificent arch was erected on Newland for the visit of Edward VII in 1907. Surmounted with ploughs and a threshing machine, it is advertising the products of local engineers Robey & Co. The postcard was published by local photogapher P Jones.

26. Horncastle area. This appears to be a bonny baby competition - there are at least seventeen of them! The card was published by Miss Blades of Horncastle c1910.

27. Lincoln Pleasure Fair at 1907, w
Market on Monks Road, now Lincoln
published by the Gainsborough Phot

is time was held on the Cattle
e. The card is posted in 1907 and

28. Burgh Le Marsh Village Fair c1905. This set of gallopers visited most fairs in the county as it was owned by Smith (Miss) and Warren of Lincoln.

29. Washingborough Show 1908 on a postcard by P. Jones of Lincoln. These cyclists look almost professional, so I assume the event had attracted entrants other than from the village.

30. Mablethorpe. A card portraying the 'Battle of Flowers' on a postcard by Bullen of Grimsby posted in 1907.

31. Mablethorpe. Clements Concert Party of 1913. According to a note on the back, the performers were Herbert Durant, Jimmy Loft, Joe Cookson, Jack Morris, Neil Francis, Fred Clifford, Lucy Clements, Jack Clements and Rob Curry.

91.93.
Arriving at Mablethorpe.

32. Mablethorpe Railway Station featured on this Doncaster Rotophoto Co card posted in 1922. The message reads *"... not ever so rowdy but the sands are glorious"*. You could still say that today, but alas the station has gone.

33. Mablethorpe - racing on the sands c1910. This must have been quite a spectacle at the time; perhaps these were the first cars some people had seen!

34. Trusthorpe Caravan Park on a Donlion of Doncaster postcard from the 1920s. Some of these look like up-market garden sheds - they certainly weren't towed by cars!

35. Skegness char-a-banc when the trip from the Clocktower to Figure 8 was just one penny! With wooden latted seats and solid tyres, it's perhaps just as well it didn't travel far.

36. Skegness's famous Jolly Fisherman, originally painted by John Hassall for a Great Northern Railway poster. This is a 'Celesque' series card published by a Tunbridge Wells firm called Photochrom. It was posted in 1909.

37. Skegness. What a wonderful Edwardian scene, except the ladies don't look much happier than the donkeys! Photographed by Thompson of Skegness, one of the entrepreneurs who made a summer living snapping holidaymakers.

SPILSBY HORSE FAIR

38. Spilsby Horse Fair on a card posted to G Ashton on a Royal Navy ship in 1910. This must have been quite a sight (and smell) judging by the number of horses.

39. Spilsby Wesleyan Chapel Sunday School celebrations of 1914, captured on a card by local photographer T. Bundock. This chapel was built in 1878 and still dominates the town centre.

40. Woodhall Spa. This is the Bardney Band appearing at the Woodhall Spa Sunday School procession on a card posted in 1906.

41. Stickford Coronation Festival 22nd June 1911. As the population of the village was only about 400 at this time, it would appear that most of them put in an appearance at the celebrations!

42. Waddington Carnival 1927 on a card published by C. & A. G. Lewis of Nottingham, though the card was not posted until 1948. Obviously a fancy dress competition is in progress, but the two children in front look distinctly unhappy about it!

Swinton, Stationer, P.O., Metheringham   *Meet of Blankney Hounds at Metheringham*

43. Metheringham. Meeting of the Blankney Hounds on a postcard by Swinton who kept the post office. The card was posted to Lincoln in March 1906.

Wesley Picnic, Ruskington.

44. Ruskington, and another chapel celebration on a card published by village photographer Peatman. Not dated, but it would appear to be Edwardian by the style of the ladies' hats!

45. Caythorpe. I have not identified this site, but I am assured it is Caythorpe. Nevertheless, it is a lovely village fair scene and the gallopers in the foreground and the swings are owned by Smith & Warren of Lincoln. The Martin's gondolas in the background also appear on other cards of Lincolnshire fairs.

46. *Rippingale 1934* is the handwritten caption on the back. This looks like a village pageant of some sort, but someone will probably remember it, as the children on the front row are probably still with us!

47. Colsterworth Braiders on a postcard posted in August 1909. The message begins *"These are maypole plaiters at Easton Park at the flower show"*. I have seen similar cards to this of Colsterworth, so I assume the village was noted for its maypole dancers. The card was published by G. Baker, the village photographer.

48. Grantham. It would seem that the lorry is part of some procession but the card is not used or dated.

BELVOIR HOUNDS AT GRANTHAM.   MAR: 19ᵗʰ 1909.

49. Grantham, and the meeting of the Belvoir Hounds on 19th March 1909. The card was posted in East Bridgford in April 1909 and addressed to Morton near Bourne. The writer says he arrived safely but has forgotten his horn and ring!

50. Grantham. The postmark is not clear, but possibly 1911, which would make this a George V coronation bonfire. The card was sent from 26 Avenue Road.

51. A local celebration at **Driby** on a card posted in August 1912. The character on the left with the fiddle under his arm would appear to be in folk costume.

52. Langrick showing the opening of the bridge over the river Witham on a postcard posted in September 1907. The message reads *"... Will and I went to London for the half day..."*!

53. South Kyme Garden Fete at the vicarage on a lazy day in Edwardian Lincolnshire.

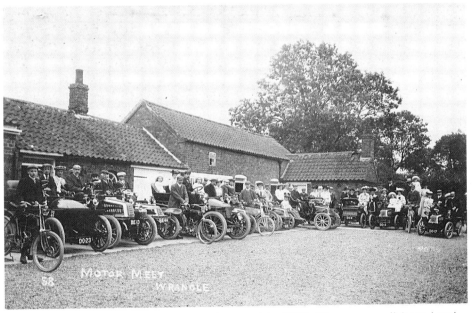

54. Wrangle motor meet on a card posted in 1905. These cars all bear local registration numbers including DO4, DO5, DO17, DO23, BE12 and BE13. The card was published by Peakome of Boston.

55. Boston May Fair on a postcard by Henson of Boston posted in the town on 15th May 1907.

56. Boston Regatta on a postcard posted in 1904. I hope some more people turned up - there are so few you can count them!

57. Donington. Village celebration of some sort, possibly the coronation of 1911, outside the *Rose & Crown* Hotel.

58. Spalding. Yet again, no clue to what is going on here. It is obviously of Edwardian vintage, but there are no flags or bunting. The photograph was taken in The Crescent with the Sessions House in the background.

59. Spalding. This band must have made quite a sound with 22 playing clarinets plus cymbals, drum and triangle. The vicar was in charge of a group of naval cadets.

60. Sutton Bridge. Coronation celebrations on a card posted in the town on 29th June 1911.